PADRE PIO'S DEVOTION TO MARY

"In the darkness, in the storms, there is nothing more reassuring than holding on tightly to our Mother, the Mother of Heaven."

PADRE PIO'S DEVOTION *to* MARY

by
Luciano Regolo

Translated from Italian by
Rev. Msgr. C. Anthony Ziccardi, S.S.L., S.T.D.

CATHOLIC BOOK PUBLISHING CORP.
New Jersey

NIHIL OBSTAT: Rev. Pawel Tomczyk, Ph.D.
Censor Librorum

IMPRIMATUR: ✠ Kevin J. Sweeney, D.D.
Bishop of Paterson

October 7, 2022

(T-154)

ISBN 978-1-953152-98-5

Printed in Korea 22 NT 1

catholicbookpublishing.com

Contents

Introduction

Our Lady's presence was a constant feature of Saint Pio's life, from its dawn to its sunset, so much so that he said, "I feel like a sailboat, propelled by the breath of the Heavenly Mother."

In 1915, Father Agostino of San Marco in Lamis noted in his *Diary*, concerning his mystic confrere, who was his penitent: "The ecstasies and the apparitions began when he was five years old, when he first thought of consecrating himself forever to the Lord, and these continued throughout his life." Among these apparitions, we can certainly also include those of the Virgin Mary. In fact, immediately afterwards, Father Agostino added in his *Diary*: "When I asked him why he had hidden these experiences for so long, he replied sincerely that he had not disclosed them because he believed them to be ordinary things that happened to all souls; in fact, one day he naively said to me, 'And you do not see Our Lady?' To my negative response, he replied, 'Surely, you say this out of holy humility!'"

Where Saint Pio felt the presence of the Mother of God most vividly and incisively was in his priestly ministry, especially during Mass and the Sacrament of Reconciliation.

Writing to his confessor on May 1, 1912, the Friar of Pietrelcina confided to him: "My Father, how well you preach this month the sweetness and beauty of Mary! In thinking of the countless benefits that this dear Mommy has bestowed on me, I am ashamed of myself for never having gazed with sufficient love upon her heart and her hand that have shared these benefits so kindly with me. Poor Mommy, how much she loves me! I have seen this once again at the dawn of this beautiful month. With what care she accompanied me to the altar this morning. It seemed to me that she had nothing else to think about except me, filling my heart with holy affections."

Then full of years and experience, Padre Pio also disclosed to a young Capuchin priest that the Virgin shared with him his mission of dispensing divine mercy: "She accompanies me into the confessional," he said, "in order that I may make myself available to my brothers. She shows me, always covered by the veil of her mercy, the innumerable souls awaiting an absolution that destroys all evil and creates all good. It is thanks to her and her desire that I have the joy of witnessing this phenomenon of grace with my own eyes and of seeing interpreted the significance of my absolution and of all the works that derive from it. I beg her to draw close to me, to suggest to me what I must say and also to suggest to my spiritual children what they must tell me. And I am sure that I am heard by her."

Furthermore, Mary of Nazareth was always the "go-to" person for his prayers, especially those he offered to summon divine intervention upon the hardships of the many needy people who turned to him. In those moments of personal conversation with the Lord, the stigmatic Friar tried to keep his "eyes on the eyes of the Heavenly Mother," being fully aware that "our prayers are worth nothing or almost nothing," whereas "they become almost omnipotent when accompanied, as in a duet, by the intercession of Our Lady."

Ultimately, Padre Pio turned his gaze to her to withstand and overcome the many and painful trials of his life. "In the darkness, in the storms," he said, "there is nothing more reassuring than holding on tightly to our Mother, the Mother of Heaven." And in her loving protection, the Comforter of the afflicted never failed him. Therefore, he endeavored to instill Marian devotion into all his spiritual children and, more generally, into those who entrusted themselves to his prayers, guaranteeing: "At the mere signal from our Blessed Mother, despair, which is the evil of our century and the cancer of society, will flee." And he predicted: "Fortunately, the present heretical currents will not destroy our faith in Our Lady, in the angels, or in the saints. Let me be clear: disbelief will lose the battle, just when, for all intents and purposes, having fired its final round of ammunition and destroyed the last sentiment of faith, it thinks it has won."

The comfort and loving presence of the Virgin Mary could certainly not be lacking in the final moments of his earthly life, on September 23, 1968. Brother Pellegrino Funicelli, who was Padre Pio's personal assistant in the final years, and therefore also his attendant that last night, revealed that, before entering into his final agony, the elderly Friar's gaze remained glued to one of the walls of his cell, where his parents' photographs were afixed, but he stated: "I see two mothers." Furthermore, the numerous witnesses to his death unanimously affirmed that the Capuchin Saint died repeating the names of Jesus and Mary over and over again.

A confrere and scholar of Saint Pio, Brother Marcellino Iasenzaniro, in one of his books, defined him as "a great lover of Our Lady." And he certainly was this. But it is also important to stress his desire to pass on this love to his spiritual children and her devotees. In 1912, to the aforementioned Father Agostino, the Friar of Pietrelcina wrote: "I would like to have a voice great enough to be able to invite sinners from all over the world to love Our Lady. But since this is not in my power, I have prayed, and I will ask my little angel to discharge this duty for me."

Padre Pio, however, did not give up on carrying out this task that was assigned to him in those contexts in which his "voice" was sufficient—starting in his friary. This was attested by Brother Pellegrino, who in a conference held in San Giovanni Rotondo in 1985 recounted: "Always and in every circumstance, as a confrere and above all as a confessor, by example and demeanor, as well as with suggestions and exhortations, he enticed me to venerate the Heavenly Mother. He exhorted me to relish the joy of loving her deeply." On one occasion, to the same confrere, Padre Pio confided: "If my spiritual children become convinced of this faith in and devotion to the Blessed Mother, I will not think that I have worked in vain in this world; and upon my death, I shall rest in peace."

Stefano Campanella
Director of Padre Pio TV

"I feel united and bound to the Son through His Mother."

Chapter 1

Our Lady of Libera, Spark of Great Love

"In thinking of the countless benefits that this dear Mommy has bestowed on me, I am ashamed of myself for never having gazed with sufficient love upon her heart and her hand that have shared these benefits so kindly with me. Poor Mommy, how much she loves me!" This is what Padre Pio wrote to Father Agostino of San Marco in Lamis in a letter dated May 1, 1912, at the commencement of the Marian month, expressing all the gratitude and immense love he had for Our Lady.

The relationship between Mary and Francesco Forgione was ignited by love from the earliest years of life of the future Saint of the Gargano region. The parish of the Forgiones in Pietrelcina, the town where Pio came into the world, on May 25, 1887, was dedicated to her, to Saint Mary of the Angels. His parents, Grazio—known as "Orazio," that is, Horace—and Peppa, went more often to the church of

Saint Anne, closer to their home, where the little one received Baptism, just one day after his birth, and eventually First Communion and Confirmation. However, the Forgione family went to Saint Mary of the Angels for the more important religious holidays and, above all, to pray in front of the seventeenth-century polychrome wooden statue depicting Our Lady of Libera, patron saint of Pietrelcina, whom Padre Pio would forever call affectionately "Our Madonnella" or "Our Little Lady."

In the tiny family home, his mother would cradle him in her arms whenever he cried and bring him before one of her small pictures of Our Lady of Libera (a sort of local "variant" of Our Lady of Graces that awaited the Friar in San Giovanni Rotondo), whispering to him: "Come, now, throw a kiss to Our Lady of Graces." This title had been conferred on Mary by the Samnites in AD 663, when the Lombard duchy of Benevento (to which Pietrelcina belonged) was freed by the Virgin's intercession from the siege and fury of the Byzantine Emperor Constans II.

The Forgione family used to sit in a semicircle around the hearth on long winter evenings. Mother Peppa would pull out a long string of beads from her apron pocket and slowly recite the rosary. The children and father Orazio answered the Marian invocations in chorus, until the eyes of the little ones began to close from sleep. The only one who remained wide awake was Francesco. The mysteries of the rosary, which Peppa recalled in fairytale tones, enchanted him. It was there, in front of the lit fireplace of the Forgione home in Pietrelcina, that Francesco's heart was set on fire for Mary. Then, when he was still a child, the beloved Heavenly Mother appeared to him, beautiful, clothed in delicate robes of the same colors as those of Our Lady of Libera. The first apparition occurred in the parish church, and he could not even let out a sound. Then he would also see her in Piana Romana, his family's country farm.

To the Virgin, Queen of Virgins, Francesco offered his virginity and his whole self. This offering was greatly appreciated, and Our Lady of Libera pleased the child with the promise of constant protection and frequent apparitions about which the Friar would keep silent until 1951 when, asked by his confessor, Father Agostino of San Marco in Lamis, Padre Pio would disclose that he had never spoken of these because he believed them to be "normal for all souls."

The "encounters" with Mary intensified over the years. Francesco, returning home from Piana Romana, would stop to collect the most beautiful and fragrant wildflowers along the way. He made bouquets of them and took them to Our Lady. Often, after serving at Mass, he would ask questions of the chief priest concerning the "Heavenly Mommy" who, from the altar, followed him with her eyes. In this way, he learned that several times over the years, since being proclaimed patron Saint of Pietrelcina, she had saved the city from many misfortunes, such as the cholera epidemic of the nineteenth century.

Francesco also learned the legend handed down about the statue of his "Little

Lady": "The sculptor, despite the assistance of other artists, was unable to finish it; the head never turned out well. The small group of sculptors decided to take a break, recharge their batteries, and seek some inspiration. When they returned to work, however, they found that the head of Our Lady had already been sculpted." This was a story that greatly moved Francesco, who fell increasingly "in love" with Our Lady of Libera. He convinced the sacristan to let him stay in the church even after closing time. He would take part with deep feeling and joy in the processions, in the songs, and in the lighting of candles in honor of the Virgin, often trying to recruit his peers. At Christmas, he was thrilled if the bagpipers came by the church to play before Our Lady of Libera.

Hints of this great love are found in the compositions he wrote at school. "On the first Sunday of August," he wrote as a boy, "as always, the feast of Our Most Holy Lady of Libera was solemnly marked by the customary pomp. The city's band played, as well as the band of the 89th regiment. The length of Umberto I Boulevard was lit up with colored lights, and in the evening there was a fireworks display. A sung Mass with instrumental accompaniment was celebrated in church, and a young priest of Paduli delivered for Our Lady a magnificent tribute that was most pleasing."

To the Virgin of Libera, Francesco entrusted his every thought, every fear, every need. In a letter to his father, who emigrated to America, he wrote on October 5, 1901: "We too, thanks be to the Lord, are well. And in a particular way, I address continuous prayers to our beautiful Virgin, so that she may protect you from all evil and return you safe and sound to us." When, at the age of sixteen, in 1903, he left Pietrelcina for the novitiate in Morcone, he brought with him two things from which he would never be separated: his rosary beads, which were a gift of his mother, and an image of Our Lady of Libera.

In Saint Mary of the Angels, Fra Pio began his apostolate. And, having been ordained a deacon, in 1909, he administered baptism for the first time to a child destined to become a priest in the Redemptorist Missionaries, the order founded by St. Alphonsus Maria Liguori. Also in Saint Mary of the Angels, in the house of "his Little Lady," on August 14, 1910, four days after his ordination to the priesthood, Padre Pio celebrated his first Mass and lived moments of intense intimacy with God, ecstasy at the foot of the altar, and the mystical experience of the fusion of hearts: his heart with that of Jesus.

Again, as when he was an altar boy, Padre Pio's eyes met in silence, full of understanding, the eyes of Our Lady of Libera, as he tasted those "heavenly delights" about which he would later write in his letters to his spiritual directors. Even when he was unable to return to his hometown, he never gave up his attachment to her. From the cell of the friary of San Giovanni Rotondo, Padre Pio ran with his mind and heart to the feet of Our Lady of Libera several times during his life. On his desk, not surprisingly, stood a copy of her precious image.

"During his illness," Father Mariano of Santa Croce di Magliano recalls, "when he woke up in the evening and often during the night, we left his room in the dim light and covered the lamp, and he was happy as the light shone on the image of Our Lady of Libera. Then he would continue his prayer until five in the morning, when he celebrated Holy Mass."

On that image Padre Pio would fix his last gaze, on the night of September 23, 1968, while his lips continued to repeat along with Jesus' name the sweet name of Mary until his heart, consumed with love, could no longer beat for her.

Throughout his life, Saint Pio constantly drew encouragement from Mary. He himself confessed: "I remain active always through the strength I draw from her." During his mystical encounters with the Virgin, he experienced the regenerating energy of the smile of Our Lady, whose beauty he praised as being "without equal even to the most beautiful things in creation."

Father Eusebio of Castelpetroso reported: "One evening, we were alone in his cell. Under his window people sang a hymn to Our Lady, whose refrain went like this: 'You are as beautiful as sun, white as the moon....' At these words, Padre Pio commented: 'If she were no more beautiful than this, then I would refuse to go to heaven.' Struck by his comment, I replied, 'But Father, what could be more beautiful than the sun and the moon?' And he, with compassion for me, added with a dialectal turn of phrase, 'Infinitely more so!' His answer was a wide smile from heaven, more eloquent than any words."

Padre Pio made the "contemplation" of Mary the fulcrum of his priesthood, so much so that he affirmed in conversations with Father Pellegrino: "In my priestly ministry, I had only one example, only one still-point: Our Lady.... I want every heart to become a Home for the Relief of Suffering, of which she must be its mistress. The promptings and glances of the Heavenly Mother suffice to give me every ability and much courage in the practice of charity towards my brothers."

Among other things, Our Lady always helped him with a mother's tenderness after every attack of the devil, right from the very first assaults in the little tower room of Pietrelcina. This is confirmed by the Diary of Father Agostino of San Marco in Lamis. Herein we learn that in Venafro, in November 1911, and in his later stay in Pietrelcina, Padre Pio, then a young priest, after terrible temptations, experienced "several ecstasies, in which there regularly appeared to him Jesus, Our Lady, and his guardian angel." Father Agostino recounts conversations, from November 28 to December 3, in which, like a lover, Padre Pio repeated several times names, such as: "Mommy," "my Mommy," "that Lady, your Mother," and "dear Mommy." In his ecstasy of Novcmber 29, he came around to saying to her, "Listen, Mommy … I love you more than all the creatures of earth and heaven … After Jesus, of course … but I love you."

Also to Father Agostino, in a letter of May 1, 1912, Padre Pio wrote pointedly: "I would like to have so strong a voice as to be able to invite sinners from all over the world to love Our Lady." One day, in his usual forthright manner, Father Pellegrino asked Padre Pio, "Why do you solve everything or have Our Lady solve everything?" He replied: "It is a matter of preference, no? But the choice was not mine." Regarding this light exchange, Father Marcellino Iasenzaniro observes: "Should we then conclude that it was Heaven itself that presented the Mother of the Lord to the Saint as the protagonist of grace and graces, and that Padre Pio—a chosen and pure creature—was but the willing instrument in those maternal hands? We really believe this to be the case."

In another letter to his spiritual father, Padre Pio explains very clearly that he sees in the Virgin the most wonderful example of faith in the Lord, because her faith does not waver even in the face of the harrowing torture of her crucified Son: "How sweet, Father, is the word cross! Here, at the foot of Jesus' cross, souls are clothed in light, they are inflamed with love; here they acquire their wings to rise to the most sublime heights. [...] Let us take care not to separate the cross from our love for Jesus: otherwise, the former without the latter would become an unbearable burden. May the Virgin of Sorrows obtain for us from her Most Holy Son the grace to enter ever more deeply into the mystery of the cross and, with her, to become intoxicated in Jesus' sufferings. The surest proof of love consists in suffering for the beloved; and after the Son of God endured so many sufferings out of pure love, there is no doubt that the cross we carry for Him becomes as lovable as love. May the Blessed Virgin obtain for us love for the cross, for sufferings, for sorrows. And may she who was the first to put into action the Gospel in all its perfection, in all its difficulty, even before it was written, obtain for us as well—she herself—the desire to follow her in this. Let us also strive, as so many chosen souls, to remain always behind the Blessed Mother, to follow forever in her footsteps, since there is no other path that leads to life, if not the one taken by Our Mother:

let us not reject this path, we who want to arrive at its destination." Padre Pio, therefore, points to the Virgin Mary as the forerunner of the way of salvation, the first soul in the procession of those willing to accompany Jesus to Calvary; about her, he writes: "I feel united and bound to the Son through His Mother."

His Marian vision was vibrant: "Let us gaze upon Mary's self-denial," he repeated. This is the concept: Our Lady becomes a rag, humble, small—in order to host Jesus in her womb. Mary's method for bringing us to Christ is to make us small, and this happens in the Sacrament of Confession. God shows us mercy when He sees that Our Lady is about to wash our rags; likewise, we "come down to size," ask the Lord to forgive our sins, and bow down before Him. This also explains the great importance that Confession held for Padre Pio, who, not surprisingly, spent many hours listening to the faithful.

"Did you pray to Our Lady for me?"

Chapter 2

Joined Inextricably to Our Lady, Between Loreto and Pompei

Saint Pio came to devotion—or, rather, to love for Our Lady—by unusual paths, indeed unfathomable. And the same may be said of his dedication to some Marian shrines, to which he was very attached, without his ever having visited them, at least not in flesh and blood. One of these places which had a special place in his heart was undoubtedly the Holy House of Loreto.

The Friar of the Gargano region always urged his spiritual children to invoke the Virgin of Loreto; and if he received pilgrims from the North, he never failed to ask, "Did you make a stop in Loreto? Did you pray to Our Lady for me?" And when they were about to set off for the return journey, he urged them to put in a visit to Mary's abode: "Pray for me and remember me to Our Lady." He would say these words in a special way that conveyed all the joy that he experienced at the thought that they might make this visit. Similarly, his disappointment was palpable if he learned that they had not stopped in Loreto, nor would they. By expressing his regret, he highlighted the good fortune that was theirs in being able go there physically, whereas the possibility of doing so was denied to him. If someone came to him, saying, "Father, I prayed for you in Loreto," this immediately put him in a good mood.

Once, Father Giuseppe Alimonti, another confrere who stood by him, recounted that Padre Pio was speaking to a pilgrim about the importance of going to the place that housed the walls within which Mary had pronounced her "yes" and had become the medium for the mystery of the Incarnation. Referring to the effect that the mere thought produced in him, Padre Pio said, "If I were to enter that house for a single instant, I would die on account of the immense feeling." This statement was to make history as an undisputable sign of the devotion that he had for the

Holy House of Loreto. To another interlocutor who hinted at a sort of comparison between Lourdes and Loreto, he replied, "Our Lady appeared in Lourdes, but in Loreto she strolls."

But if Padre Pio was never able to cross the threshold of the House of Loreto, one naturally wonders: how did he manage to cultivate such immense devotion to the dark-skinned Virgin who is venerated there? A page from the chronicle of the friary of San Giovanni Rotondo offers a fascinating explanation. For May 20, 1958, we find the following entry: "Brother Gianmaria, who resides at the Holy House, came and said that in the evening, sometimes earlier and sometimes later, depending on the season, at 7:00 or 7:15 or 8:00 or 8:25 or sometimes even around 9:00 or 1:00, Padre Pio knocks on the door of the Holy House. Friar Gianmaria reports that Padre Pio confirmed this to our Provincial Minister Father Raffaele from Sant'Elia a Pianisi.

"Brother Gianmaria also recounts that once, while he was standing in front of

Our Lady, he addressed this prayer to her: 'My Lady, if it is true that Padre Pio comes here, to your house, let him come now!' And at that very instant he heard the knock of Padre Pio on the door. This happened also another time. We point out that Brother Gianmaria is a reliable and credible person. He affirms that today he said to Padre Pio: 'Father, continue to come and visit us in the Holy House.' And Padre Pio started laughing, nodding yes. The time noted by Brother Gianmaria matches the time in which Padre Pio, after the departure of his closest associates, remains alone…"

Other testimonies were collected from this sanctuary located in the Marche region, such as that of Father Remigio of Cavedine, a Capuchin friar and priest, who for many years was the guardian of the Holy House of Loreto and known to his confreres as a man of great piety and devotion to the Virgin. Every evening, at exactly nine o'clock, he would recite the rosary in the Holy House. He himself reported that at the exact moment in which he began Padre Pio would arrive and remain there for the duration of the prayer. One of the spiritual sons of the Saint of the Gargano region, Giovanni Bardazzi, better known to all as "Giovanni from Prato," who passed away in 1997 at about the age of ninety, being on a pilgrimage in Loreto, asked Father Remigio, "How could I too see Padre Pio here?" The religious brother replied, "I don't know if the Lord will allow you to see him, but look at the chains placed on the sides of the barriers. As he passes, you will see them move." The story of these and other "bi-locations in Loreto" soon went around the world.

Another Marian sanctuary with which Saint Pio had a particular bond was Pompei. On account of his attachment to the Queen of the Rosary, who is venerated there, the Friar of the stigmata also became friends with the founder of the sanctuary of Pompei, the future Blessed Bartolo Longo. In a youthful letter from Padre Pio, not surprisingly, there is found in the list of his particular devotions, which he practiced every day, the novena to Our Lady of Pompei. Padre Pio visited this Marian sanctuary at least three times: in 1901, when as a boy he went there with some schoolmates; in November 1911, accompanied by Father Evangelista, superior of the friary of Venafro; on January 3, 1917, when he was on leave from military service. During these three visits, his devotion to the Queen of the Rosary was strengthened. In his correspondence, he makes various references to Our Lady of Pompei. In a letter sent to Father Agostino of San Marco in Lamis, his spiritual director, for example, he requests of him "the great kindness of beginning as soon as possible the three novenas to the Virgin of Pompei, with the daily recitation, during this period, of the full rosary." He requested the same of his spiritual daughters.

He had not yet turned fourteen when he went to Pompei for the first time, probably in May 1901. We find confirmation of this pilgrimage in a letter dated October 5, 1901, by the young Francesco to his father, who had emigrated to the United

States in search of work. Grazio, in fact, learned of his son's visit to the sanctuary and complained to his wife: while he was overseas breaking his back for his family, he wrote to her, they were squandering money. Francesco tried to assuage him as best he could by promising to dedicate himself more assiduously to his studies: "Regarding your complaint to mom about my going to Pompei, you are right .... It is true that I wasted a few dollars, but now I promise you to earn them by studying. In fact, now I find myself under the guidance of a new teacher, and I realize that I am progressing day by day, so that both mom and I are very happy."

Francesco made the journey from Pietrelcina to Pompei, in stages, aboard a coach with his teacher Angelo Caccavo and seven other students. It was not a normal vehicle, but the "sciaraballo," that is, a wagon with lateral and transversal wooden seats, capable of carrying 14 to 15 people. This was not a mere school trip, but a "fellowship," that is, a group of pilgrims headed to Pompei, either on the first Sunday of October or on May 8, feast days on which the supplication to the Virgin of the Rosary is solemnly prayed. Before leaving, the "fellowship" went to the parish church, participated in Mass, and having received the blessing from the priest, they set out at dusk for the chosen destination.

Padre Pio would return to Pompei as a young priest towards the middle of November 1911. He had been in the friary of Venafro for less than a month. On his way to Naples with the guardian of the friary, Father Evangelista of San Marco in Lamis, for a medical appointment scheduled for the afternoon, he went the next day together with the superior to the sanctuary of Pompei. The details of the visit are found in a report by Brother Serafico of Riccia as transmitted by Father Gerardo of Flumeri in his book *The Stop of Padre Pio in Venafro*. The report reads thus: "After the medical exam, it got to be late, and they went to sleep in a hotel.... In the morning, they decided to go to Pompei to visit Our Lady. Thus, each celebrated a

Holy Mass, one serving the other in turn. Later they stopped in a church to give thanks to the Lord, and then they visited all the works of the sanctuary and arrived around 2....They went to a restaurant and returned to their friary."

Five years later, on December 30, 1916, Padre Pio, who had previously been called up for military service in the Great War, was put on sick leave for six months. He sent a similar notification to Father Paolino of Casacalenda, his superior at the friary of San Giovanni Rotondo, to Father Augustine, and to two of his spiritual daughters: "Hospital of the Holy Trinity. Thanks be to God! This morning I had my medical exam.... They limited themselves to granting me six months of convalescence. Patience! Better this than nothing. I hope to be discharged this evening. Tomorrow morning, God willing, I will go to visit Our Lady of Pompei. After a quick stop in Pietrelcina, I will return immediately to my residence (San Giovanni Rotondo). As far as my health is concerned, I feel terrible."

In 1921, although he never returned to the sanctuary of Campania, Padre Pio was already on friendly terms with Longo, so much so that he wrote him an affectionate letter on November 11 of the same year: "O Soul Beloved by God, may Jesus always be all yours. May He always assist you with His watchful grace and make you worthy of His divine embraces. With these very sincere wishes, which I express before Jesus and the Virgin Mother, I respond to your most welcome correspondence that reached me yesterday. I am sorry to learn of your niece's illness, and I hope that the Blessed Virgin will soon restore her to health. I do not approve at all of your wife's hesitation in regard to the small house in the Valley of Pompei for the budding institution, and this makes me fear greater evils. And so, may your lady be more generous, and be assured that the Virgin will not leave without recompense so beautiful a deed done in her honor. With the greatest esteem, I greet you fraternally and commend myself to your prayers."

It is likely that this letter from Padre Pio, in response to Longo's letter, refers to the establishment of the Home for the Daughters of the Imprisoned, which would be launched the following year in 1922. The Pompeian founder had asked the future Saint for advice, setting forth for him the various issues. And Padre Pio, with his typical directness, urged Bartolo to follow his intuition and not to pay attention to contrary opinions, even when they came from his wife. In any case, the letter shows the intense closeness and spiritual understanding between the two, so much so that the Friar does not hesitate to wish Longo "divine embraces." And a further sign of this is Padre Pio's shipment to Pompei of a French image of Our Lady of the Rosary, behind which he wrote in his own hand: "For the Knight Commander Bartolo Longo. May Mary always guard you with her maternal glance and comfort you in your afflictions." Love for the Virgin was a strong bond between the two.

Cesira Cavalli Angelini, spiritual daughter of Blessed Longo and devotee of

Padre Pio, in April 1922 was struck by a severe bout of a pernicious fever. Hence, she turned to Bartolo and asked him to pray for her recovery. Her spiritual director, ready, sent her a "relic" of the Friar with the stigmata, which had recently been given to him. As soon as the relic reached her and she had it in her hands, her temperature dropped. Cesira immediately wrote to Bartolo to tell him the good news. The response, dated May 1, 1922, was not long in coming: "Most esteemed and dearest daughter in Jesus Christ, from your letter of April 22 I learned with great pleasure that the fever left you as soon as you had in your hands the relic that I sent you of the living Holy Padre Pio. We thank the Lord who deigns to show us mercy even through His servants on earth. Although I have been ill for several days with severe constipation and some inflammation in one eye, nevertheless on May 8 (Feast of Our Lady of Pompei, *editor*) I will not fail to pray and have others pray for you and for your children, so that Our Lady may grant all those graces you desire. And I will tell Our Lady to keep you safe and make you a Saint in order that you may eternally enjoy God, who loves us so much. With a thousand greetings and blessings, I remain very humbly and affectionately yours in Jesus Christ."

Note the flattering opinion that the two great "champions of the rosary" of the early twentieth century had about each other: Bartolo Longo considered Padre Pio a "living Saint," and the latter considered the Pompeian founder a "soul of God."

The lure that the sanctuary of Pompei exercised upon Padre Pio is revealed by another event. On September 20, 1968, for the fiftieth anniversary of the stigmata, he was offered a basket of flowers with fifty red roses, one for each year of "mystical crucifixion." With his hand, wounded by love, the Saint took a rose from the basket and handed it to a spiritual son of his who was going to Naples. He instructed him to take it to Pompei and place it in front of the painting of Our Lady of the Rosary. That rose, having reached its destination, unlike the others that surrounded it, did not wither. On September 23, the day of

Padre Pio's death, the bishop of Pompei, Aurelio Signora, seeing that rose was still fresh and fragrant, placed it among the most cherished and precious articles of the sanctuary. This prodigious event was recalled fifty years later, from November 16 to 25, 2018, with a pilgrimage of the reliquary containing the rose offered by Saint Pius to the Queen of the Rosary and the painting of Our Lady of Pompei in San Giovanni Rotondo, as part of the jubilee celebrations for the first centenary of the Saint's reception of the stigmata and the fiftieth anniversary of his blessed *transitus* (passing).

A very detailed and compelling reconstruction of the last tribute paid to the Virgin of Pompei by Padre Pio, who was almost on the verge of death, is found in the book by Brother Tarcisio of Cervinara *Padre Pio and Our Lady*: "On September 20, 1968, on the occasion of the 50th anniversary of the visible impression of the stigmata on his flesh, someone from Naples offered Padre Pio a bundle of red roses. The stigmatic of the Gargano region, visibly moved, took a rose from the bundle, placed it in the hands of that kind heart, and said to him: 'Bring this rose to Our Lady of Pompei for me!'"

The lucky donor, Brother Tarcisio continues, "was delighted with the assignment. He brought the rose to Pompei. He asked a religious sister of the sanctuary to place the rose sent by Padre Pio in front of the painting of Our Lady. The sister, at the sound of that name, joyfully added that flower with fervent piety to the others that had been placed in front of Mary." On September 23, "when the Seraphim of Pietrelcina had already flown off to heaven, the sister, removing the flowers before Our Lady, noticed that, while all the others had withered, Padre Pio's rose was still fresh, scented, fragrant: closing up, however, it had become once again a sweet and graceful bud. This was a sign, concludes Brother Tarcisio, "given by heaven to indicate that that bud had opened up in the temple above to remain an immortal rose before the celestial throne of Mary."

"I am cured! Our Lady has healed me!"

Chapter 3

The Intercessor of Many Miracles Receives a Miracle from Our Lady of Fatima

Padre Pio showed constant and special veneration for Our Lady of Fatima and for her Immaculate Heart. From May to October 1917, when the Friar was only twenty years old, the Virgin had appeared in the countryside of the small Portuguese parish to Jacinta, Francisco, and Lucia, three little shepherds who had brought their sheep there to graze far from town, just as Francesco Forgione had done in Pietrelcina when he was little.

All of Europe at that time was severely tested by the end of the First World War, a useless carnage caused by violent nationalism and by the greed of large business and Masonic lobbies. Our Lady entrusted to the little shepherds of Fatima extraordinary messages also about the future of the world. But she invited them especially to understand and make others understand the true meaning of the cross, the instrument of God's immense love for men and women.

The Virgin highlighted for the three children the urgent need to rediscover clearly the loving sacrifice of Jesus and to learn from her (hence, the symbol of the Immaculate Heart of Mary) the right disposition towards God: full conversion. Sincere love for Jesus leads to imitating what He lavished on the whole world and therefore to knowing how to suffer for others, taking on the burden of sins, even those we have not ourselves committed, because believers are, through their bond with Christ, our God and brother, one body. Father Ennio Innocenti wrote: "It is Catholic dogma that redeemed humanity is one body, a mystical body, in which each person, without losing his or her own identity, is in solidarity with everyone else. Our Lady came to remind us of this and to teach us to live our vocation with the same sentiments of her heart."

This, which is perhaps the most important invitation made by the Holy Virgin in Fatima, was not grasped fully in its most precious significance. Pius XII wanted to recall it in 1943 with his encyclical letter *Mystici Corporis*, underlining the importance of "accepting the hardships and travails of this life as from the hands of God." Paul VI did the same by going on a pilgrimage and giving an engaging speech in Fatima fourteen years later. In 1982 John Paul II also went to the Portuguese sanctuary; and on the eve of that journey, he delivered strong words on the spiritual lesson to be grasped in the messages entrusted to the little shepherds. He said, "We must prepare ourselves to undergo not too far in the future very great trials which will demand of us the willingness to give up even our lives [on May 13 of the same year John Paul II would himself be attacked in St. Peter's Square, *editor*] and total dedication to Christ and through Christ. With your prayers and mine, it is possible to attenuate this tribulation, but it is no longer possible to avert it completely because only in this way can the Church be effectively renewed. How many times has the renewal of the Church sprouted forth from blood! This time too it will not be different. We must be strong, prepare ourselves, trust in Christ and in His Most Holy Mother, and be very, very assiduous in praying the rosary."

Various Mariologists, such as René Laurentin, have highlighted the connections between the many Mariophanies that have occurred in different eras and places. They have put into relief the delicate yet strong thread that seems to unite La Salette, Lourdes, and Fatima, as if each of these apparitions corresponded to the same eternal, tireless maternal impulse to awaken consciences and to direct her children towards the right path. The apostolate of Padre Pio had this same effect as he was encouraged from an early age by his Heavenly Mother. Identification with Christ's sacrifice of love on the cross was made visible by the Saint of the Gargano region with his stigmata and with all the physical pains of the Passion, including the sweating of blood. In the same way, he lived and spread, through the cenacles and the prayer groups which he encouraged, the practice of praying the rosary as the most powerful weapon against the evils of his time. Padre Pio becomes a living example of that daily *Magnificat* which must be the true faith, which says yes to Our Lady and Jesus, like the three children of Fatima, who offered themselves as victims of love for the sake of the salvation of that mystical body of which even Christians seem to have forgotten its existence, distracted as they are by the growing materialism, by the many contemporary false myths. Entrust to the Immaculate Heart of Mary those who knock on the door, since these before others have put their trust there. Padre Pio, inviting Father Pellegrino to be captivated by the grace of Our Lady, said to him: "She is a true artist, a true mermaid in winning and conquering her children. Her charm is without tricks. She is truly beautiful; she is really good. You will see that once you are captivated by her, you will have the courage to throw yourself into the sea or to throw yourself into the fire."

To Father Pellegrino Funicelli, Padre Pio pointed out the Virgin Mary as an anchor of salvation, in life and in death, as "the stand-in for the mercy of God on earth." He also revealed to his confrere, at a time when even within the Church there were those who were devaluing the Sacrament of Reconciliation, that the Holy Virgin herself accompanied him into the confessional: "Our Heavenly Mother is too much in the shadows, like all mothers. I beg her to draw close to me, to suggest to me what I must say and also to suggest to my spiritual children what they must tell me. And I am sure that I am heard by her. It is said that any natural love leads to heroic and admirable deeds. Could we be astonished, then, if we truly appreciate what source of charity is the Heavenly Mother?"

Padre Pio founded prayer groups throughout the world. The source of this fervor was the "call to prayer" of Pope Pius XII on October 27, 1940, in the midst of World War II and in conjunction with the messages entrusted by Our Lady to the little shepherds of Fatima in 1917. The "atoning" and redemptive logic of identifying with Jesus through love prompted, in fact, Pope Pacelli to appeal to believers to create a "choir of prayers," as Our Lady had asked the three Portuguese children. What was the goal? To encourage prayer as frequent and intense contact with God through the intercession of His Mother. "We order that all over the world, on November 24," announced Pius XII, "public prayers be raised up with Us to God. And We are confident that all the children of the Church, with a willing soul, will satisfy Our desires, in such manner as to form an immense choir of prayers, which, rising up and penetrating the heavens, will gain the favor and mercy of God."

Following this appeal, the Friar of Pietrelcina went to work with all his heart, starting to organize prayer groups, which he wanted to be "nurseries of faith and hearths of love," in which Christ himself had to be present. These groups had to be approved by the bishop and directed by a priest.

Having identified the points of contact between the revelations of Our Lady in Portugal and the prayer apostolate of the Saint of Pietrelcina, we can also appreciate better the devotion he had for the image of the Virgin of Fatima. Saint Pio gave expression to this devotion by daily kneeling and praying in front of a large representation of her surrounded by lighted candles in the small sanctuary dedicated to her inside the friary. But above all he credited Our Lady for having preserved his life.

In 1959 the Italian Bishops Conference announced a year of prayer in preparation for the new decade. To mark the event, the statue of Mary, the "Pilgrim Virgin," as she appeared to the Portuguese shepherd children, was taken from the sanctuary of Fatima on April 25 of that year and brought to various cities in Italy. On the same day, Padre Pio fell ill and had to stay in bed on account of acute, oozing pleurisy. There was also talk of a malignant tumor that left little hope of his survival, but this remained a rumor that was never confirmed.

In May 1959 the future Saint's physical condition had so deteriorated that he could no longer even celebrate Holy Mass in the church but did so in his room. From his room, through an intercom, he listened to the services that were held in the church; afterwards, in the evening he addressed a short speech to the faithful, concluding with a blessing. On July 1st and 2nd of the same year in San Giovanni Rotondo, the celebrations for the consecration of the new church took place with great solemnity, with Cardinal Tedeschini and Archbishop Carta in attendance, but Padre Pio could not be present. In the chronicle, Father Raffaele from Sant'Elia a Pianisi recounts: "On July 1, with the permission of the guardian and in order not to burden the community, he tried that morning to go and celebrate Mass in the Home for the Relief of Suffering, and so he went there; but as soon as Mass was over, weak as he was, his strength failed him. He experienced dizziness and a sort of fainting spell. He had to stop at the clinic and took to bed in a very private room, where he remained for two days continuously cared for by his religious confreres. This was the physical condition of Padre Pio when the statue of Our Lady of Fatima arrived."

As a sign of affection for and devotion to the stigmatic Friar, the Italian Bishops Conference decided to have the statue of the Pilgrim Mother also pass through San Giovanni Rotondo. It arrived there on August 5, the forty-first anniversary of the Friar's transverberation (the mystical piercing of the heart), brought by a helicopter from Foggia. In prior days, Padre Pio, in the evening address that he gave by microphone from his cell, urged the faithful to prepare themselves spiritually for the visit of the Heavenly Mother, "the sea through which we arrive at the shores of eternal splendor in the kingdom of dawn." There was a whole day of prayer in front of the sacred statue that came from Portugal. The following morning, August 6, the feast of the Transfiguration, the statue, before being carried around the wards of the Home for the Relief of Suffering that had been inaugurated three years earlier and then transferred by helicopter from the roof of the hospital, was taken first to the sacristy of the friary church. The future Saint, sitting on a chair, had himself brought there. With great emotion, he leaned over to kiss the statue and placed his rosary, which he had received as a gift from one of the prayer groups, into the hands of Our Lady. Then he was taken back to his cell.

The helicopter pilot who was to bring the statue back to Foggia and his second-in-command went to the Friar to receive his blessing. A little later, he heard the cheers of the crowd and the sound of the aircraft taking off from the hospital roof. The friars who accompanied Padre Pio to a balcony of the church said that he, as the helicopter lifted off, whispered in tears: "Mother, I was sick during your visit to Italy. Are you leaving now without healing me?"

The helicopter was moving away from San Giovanni Rotondo when suddenly the second-in-command, responding to an irresistible and inexplicable impulse, asked to go back and circle the friary three times as a greeting to Padre Pio. In that same instant, according to Father Francesco Napolitano, an eyewitness to the event, the future Saint felt a shiver throughout his body. He was pervaded by a ray of light and, weeping, cried out: "I am cured! Our Lady has healed me!" In fact, according to various witnesses, for a long time he never felt so healthy and vigorous as after the departure of the statue of the Pilgrim Madonna from San Giovanni Rotondo.

"Thank the Virgin of Fatima for me," he later wrote. "The very day she left here, I felt well again. I returned to celebrating Mass three days ago."

The link between the Saint and Our Lady of Fatima has been enriched more recently with a new detail: in a report for Padre Pio TV, Jacinta Pereira Marto, niece of Francisco and Jacinta, now both canonized, affirmed that her father, João Marto, who died in 2000 at 94, the fifth of the seven children of Manuel and Olimpia, the parents of the two holy shepherds, was a great devotee of Saint Pio, and he always carried an image of the Friar of Pietrelcina in his wallet.

"Thank the Lord for the special grace He has granted you."

Chapter 4

Travels and Dialogues in Spirit with the Queen of Heaven and Court of Angels

By a strange coincidence the home parish of Padre Pio, Saint Mary of the Angels, was dedicated to Our Lady as the queen of heavenly creatures just like the basilica of Assisi, linked to the mystical experience of St. Francis, the holy "poor man," beacon of humility and love, who almost seven centuries earlier was "associated" by means of the stigmata to Jesus' Passion. This aspect of Our Lady (that is, as "Queen of Angels") moved the Saint of the Gargano region to special fervor. It is striking that in the spiritual journey and apostolate of Saint Pio, not only the Holy Virgin but also her heavenly court, that is, the angels, almost entirely forgotten even among the Catholics of his time, had a pivotal, if not decisive, role as a constant source of inspiration and as a center of gravity for his loving devotion. The association of Mary with the angels is yet another dimension of Saint Pio's special connection to Fatima, in addition to the total humility and poverty that joined the mystical experience of the three little shepherds of Portugal to that of Padre Pio.

It should not be forgotten, in fact, that in 1915, before the apparition of Our Lady, the angel of Portugal appeared to Francisco, Jacinta, and Lucia. It was this creature, "a young man of fourteen or fifteen, who was whiter than snow and whom the sun made transparent as crystal, a being of great beauty," that caused the children to marvel at the notion of expiation, a topic that seemed instantly to Lucia to be complicated. Our Lady herself, then, according to what Lucia reported, would ask them shortly thereafter: "Do you want to offer yourselves to God to atone for sins and to ask for the conversion of sinners?"

Our Lady of Fatima, therefore, was preceded by an angel, thus pointing to that path of listening and constant contact with these “soldiers” of Heaven, guardians of souls, that would mark in a particular way the work of Saint Pio. Father Alessio Parente stressed: “In the gospel story, the angels occupy an important place. And the Virgin Mary, when she was first called to participate in the Incarnation of God’s Son and the salvation of humankind, was contacted by an angel to obtain her assent to God’s will. Although the angels were at the service of Padre Pio [to obtain graces, *editor*], they were under the authority of their “Queen,” without whose permission they could do nothing. By means of prayer and his special devotion to the Virgin, he received many graces on others’ behalf; but in the stewardship of God’s gifts and graces, Padre Pio was helped by the angels. Hence, behind all of Padre Pio’s wonderful charisms, behind his singular spirituality, behind his gift for bilocation and his closeness to the angels, Our Lady was at work, caring for him tenderly as a mother cares for her child.”

The experiences of the little shepherds of Fatima, like those of the Saint of Pietrelcina, also constitute today a reminder to believers not to neglect praying to the angels as powerful helpers on their spiritual journey. Although nearly forgotten ethereal beings, they are formidable allies that are able to provide tangible daily support, so much so that Saint Pio counseled his spiritual children who found it difficult to reach him to send him every request by means of their guardian angel. And there is plenty of evidence that these "messages" were successful.

As Benedict XVI said on October 2, 2011, the Feast of the Guardian Angels, to a large crowd gathered at St. Peter's: "There are angels, and a guardian angel accompanies everyone from birth to death, because God loves every person in his or her uniqueness and protects him or hcr ceaselessly. From birth until the hour of death, every human life is surrounded by their constant protection. And the angels encircle as a 'crown' Our Lady." Explaining how Our Lady was behind the closeness of the Friar of Pietrelcina to the angels, Father Alessio Parente said: "How many times I heard this prayer from the mouth of Padre Pio: 'Oh, sweetest Mary, Mother of priests, mediatrix and dispenser of all graces, I pray to you from the bottom of my heart....' From these words we deduce that, if the angels followed the orders entrusted to them to obtain graces, they did not do so without the consent of the Queen of the Angels, who exercises authority over them."

Two young men, spiritual sons of Padre Pio, reported to the Saint that they heard, while they were on a beach in the Gulf of Manfredonia, strange sounds coming from the Gargano region, voices singing the litanies of Our Lady and "they seemed not earthly, but rather a choir of singular beauty, never heard before, a music capable of transporting and elevating their spirits." The Friar of Pietrelcina replied, "You fools, do you not understand? This was the angels praising Our Lady from above the friary. Thank the Lord for the special grace He has granted you."

Margherita Cassano, another spiritual daughter of the Saint, reported in 1969 that once, having asked Padre Pio if it was true that the rosary recited by several persons together had greater value, since she often had no alternative but to pray it alone in her home, received from him this reply: "Why do you not recite the rosary with your guardian angel? You entrust the *Hail Mary* to him, and Holy Mary shall put it to your account. The *Hail Mary*, as Saint Luke told us, is God's greeting to Mary, placed on the lips of an angel; hence, it is a good and beautiful thing if our guardian angels say it with us."

The angels and Our Lady also assisted the Friar of Pietrelcina in his "bilocations," his journeys in spirit beyond physical barriers and over long distances to help needy souls. This can be seen from the first documented bilocation which was described in February 1905 by Padre Pio himself. At the time, he was eighteen years of age and was immersed in his studies at the friary of Sant'Elia a Pianisi, in the province of Campobasso. He wrote down on a sheet of paper from a notebook the following lines, which note he then gave to Father Agostino, who stored it away: "Some days ago, an unusual event happened to me. I was in choir with Brother Anastasio at about 11:00 PM on the 18th day of last month. Suddenly, I found myself far away in a stately home, where the father was dying while his child was being born. Then Mary Most Holy appeared and said to me: 'I entrust this creature to you; she is a precious stone in a rough state. Work it, polish it, make it as shiny as possible, because one day I want to adorn it.' I said, 'How is this possible, if I am still a poor cleric, and I do not know if I will have the fortune and joy of being a priest someday? And even if I become a priest, how will I, being far from here, be able to care for this little girl?' Our Lady added, 'Do not doubt. It will be she who will come to you, but first you will meet her in St. Peter's....' After that, I found myself in choir again."

The little girl was the Marquise Giovanna Rizzani Boschi from Udine, mother-in-law of the actress Giovanna Ralli. In 1923, the Marquise became the spiritual daughter of Padre Pio and subsequently an important collaborator in the construction of the Home for the Relief of Suffering. In this written note from his youth, the Saint himself left unwitting proof of having witnessed in spirit, while he was physically in Molise, the birth of the noblewoman and the simultaneous death of her father, Giovanni Battista Rizzani, in their palace in Via Deciani in Udine.

Both events did, in fact, happen on the night of January 18, 1905. Despite the advanced state of her pregnancy, Giovanna's mother, Leonilde Serrao, was at her husband's bedside caring for him. At one point, she had to leave him in order to try to quiet the dogs that were barking unusually in the courtyard below. While on the stairs, she was overtaken by labor pangs, and she gave birth in precarious conditions, helped by the only person present at that moment, the family butler. The birth went well, and the woman found the strength to take the baby, Giovanna Rizzani Boschi, into her arms, go up the stairs, and return to the room of her husband, who expired shortly thereafter. Leonilde said she saw, during her labor, in front of her and in the corridors of the house, a Capuchin friar with a reassuring appearance. She thought it was a hallucination caused by the pain. But the writing kept by Father Agostino, of which she obtained a copy years later, revealed the real reason for what she saw.

Moreover, the "prophecy" of Our Lady recorded by the young Padre Pio also came true. Leonilde, in fact, as a widow moved to Rome, where her parents lived and where her daughter grew up. In 1922, Giovanna, then seventeen, was experiencing doubts of faith. So, in order to speak with a priest, on a sultry summer afternoon, she went with a friend to St. Peter's. But there were, however, no priests in the basilica's confessionals. Suddenly, she saw a friar walking down the aisle. She ran after him and asked to talk. They spoke for a long time. Giovanna would have liked to arrange another meeting, but the Capuchin disappeared, without either she or her friend having seen him depart by the only "humanly possible" route. The guards to whom they turned for information told them that there had never been any friars there. Giovanna continued to struggle with her inner questions, wishing to meet another priest capable of "touching" her heart like that friar.

A year later, hearing about Padre Pio for the first time and acting on a mysterious impulse, she signed up for a pilgrimage to San Giovanni Rotondo, together with an aunt and friends. The Marquise Giovanna would later give this account: "As he passed by, Padre Pio stopped in front of me. He looked into my eyes, and smiling he said to me, 'Giovanna, I know you. You were born the same day your father died.' After telling her that he was the Capuchin who had heard her confession in St. Peter's, calming her doubts about the faith, he concluded, saying, 'When you were about to be born, Our Lady took me to Udine, to your family's palace. She let me witness your father's death, and then she told me to take care of you. You have been entrusted to me by the Virgin, and I must concern myself for your soul.'"

Many times, while praying to Our Lady, Padre Pio would withdraw in spirit. And in those same moments, many of his spiritual children were helped by the angels: some fell asleep behind the wheel only to find themselves with their cars parked in front of the friary of San Giovanni Rotondo, without knowing how they got there safe and sound; others were watched over during a serious illness by someone who came from heaven. The stories abound, as also the testimonies of those who, on the other side of the world, saw Padre Pio suddenly appear with an angel beside him. The Virgin, therefore, listened to Padre Pio; and she and her court were the essential resource in his unrelenting mission of love for neighbor.

It was so, starting with his priestly service. Enrico Cerioni, a Sardinian living in Rome, wrote as follows to Brother Daniel Natale, after having stayed in San Giovanni Rotondo: "While I was waiting with the faithful for Padre Pio to come to the church to celebrate Holy Mass, I saw two rows of angels coming out of the sacristy before him. The Priest had Our Lady beside him. He approached the altar, while the Mother of God remained at his side." Cerioni ends the letter by asking Brother Daniel to ask the Friar of the stigmata if what he saw was only imagination or reality. Padre Pio, receiving into his hands the letter from his confrere and running through it with his finger, briefly confirmed: "This part regarding the presence of Our Lady and the angels is just so."

Chapter 5

Our Lady of Graces and the Weapon of the Rosary

In the friary of the Capuchins of San Giovanni Rotondo, Padre Pio was always seen walking around with a rosary in his hands. His was not only a continuous prayer to the Virgin, but with her he shared every sigh, whether it was of serenity or of need and suffering. "Love Our Lady and make her to be loved by others," he exhorted, "Always recite the rosary." Stefano Campanella wrote: "No one will ever know for certain how many full rosaries (at the time, consisting of fifteen decades) Padre Pio recited per day." A series of witnesses suggest to us about thirty-three. The only certainty is that he never let go of his rosary beads, even when he had to wash his hands, preferring to wash one at a time. A young confrere, who could not grasp the point of the ceaseless repetition of prayers using the same formulas, acknowledged to others that he was admonished by Padre Pio with these enlightening words: "You, who consider the rosary as a prayer suitable only for old ladies, take these beads and reevaluate them, precisely because of their apparently extraordinary uselessness, as a 'little tool' that opens the gates of heaven."

Another friar who asked him, "Father, why do you always recite the rosary but not other prayers?" The stigmatic Capuchin replied, "Because Our Lady has never denied me a grace that I requested through the recitation of the rosary." To one of his spiritual daughters, he recommended it as a privileged tool of self-defense from the attacks of the devil. "Let us be careful," he told her, "Let us always keep this weapon in hand and stay watchful, because the enemy does not sleep. Let us flee from even the shadow of sin." One day Father Guglielmo Alimonti, future coordinator of the Abruzzo Prayer Groups, hoping to please his venerable confrere, told him, "Father, yesterday I prayed thirty complete rosaries." He hoped to receive a compliment or a word of approval, but Padre Pio replied, "So few?"

By word and deed, he was a great and tireless apostle of the rosary. He always carried it with him, wrapped around his hand or arm, like an ornament of the soul, a powerful shield. The rosary was by far his favorite prayer, at any time of the day and during the night. In many photos one can see the Saint with his right hand hidden in his pocket, where he always kept his rosary beads. He exhorted everyone: "Love Our Lady and pray the rosary, because the rosary is the weapon against the evils of the world."

The image before which he often addressed to the Heavenly Mother his own prayers, entrusting to her the anxieties of his heart in his final years, was that of the Virgin of Graces in the wonderful mosaic in San Giovanni Rotondo. He did this day and night in the loggia of the church where he spent many hours in deep prayer. He himself disclosed this in his message to the faithful on May 5, 1957, the first anniversary of the inauguration of the Home for the Relief of the Suffering: "May Most Holy Mary of Graces, who is the queen to whom we manifest our love every day and from whom we request maternal help, always reign as sovereign in the city that will rise around her Temple, and may she assist us all."

The mosaic replicates the ancient and extraordinary painting closely linked to the history of the friary of San Giovanni Rotondo. Here, already during the eighteenth century, the Capuchins jealously guarded a painting of the Virgin of Graces, before which they offered special prayers every day. The painting was then transferred for a certain period to another church of the city, the church of Saint Nicholas, when, in 1866, the friary was suppressed.

In the first twenty years of the 1900s, Our Lady of Graces was successfully invoked to end a persistent drought that had devastated the local populace, and this further strengthened devotion to her. With the definitive reopening of the friary in 1909, and the return of the Capuchin friars there, they demanded that the painting be restored to the friary, and they came to an agreement with the people: every year, on August 31, the painting would be brought to the village for the patronal celebrations, but on September 10 it would return in procession to the friary.

This was just before the arrival of Padre Pio to the Gargano region. Gelsomino Del Guercio wrote: "The scattered flowers of the veneration of Our Lady of Graces are destined to multiply in the garden of the spirituality of the Friar of Pietrelcina. Devotion to the Virgin, especially to Our Lady of Graces, will be an indispensable part of Padre Pio's life and of his teachings." It was the Saint himself who hinted several times that all his work was guided by the loving protection of Our Lady. One day, Father Tarcisio of Cervinara asked him, "Does Our Lady ever come to your cell?" And he responded, "You should rather ask me when, if ever, she has left my cell!"

Whenever he was told about some serious difficulty, he almost always replied that he would pray to the Heavenly Mother, just as whenever he was thanked for a benefit obtained, he always replied: "Let us thank Our Lady!" Even to those who pointed out to him his inexhaustible strength in carrying a heavy, daily load, he replied that the Mother of God was the source of all his energy: "What could I manage to do without her?" Moreover, Saint Pio explained to Father Pellegrino clearly that all this was very reasonable, since "after all, it is she, Our Lady, who transmits to us a ray of God's immensity and of His divine attributes." One day another confrere asked Padre Pio, "What shall I do to become a saint?" He responded, "You will sprout wings … if you are devoted to Our Lady."

As mentioned, Padre Pio fixed his last glance upon the image of Our Lady of Libera, patroness of his hometown and the mother of his life. In the coffin, there were placed in his hands rosary beads, his dearest companion. On the door of his cell, number 5, there remained penned a maxim from Saint Bernard, shedding light on his entire life: "Mary is the whole reason for my hope."

Reflections and Prayers of Padre Pio concerning the Virgin Mary

Prayers

1.

O Mary,
sweetest mother
of priests,
mediatrix and dispenser
of all graces,
from the bottom of my heart
I beg you, I beseech you
and I entreat you to thank
today, tomorrow, always,
Jesus, the blessed fruit of
your womb.

2.

My Mother Mary,
lead me with you
into the grotto of Bethlehem
and let me plunge
into contemplation
of that which,

being great and sublime,
is to unfold
in the silence
of this great and beautiful night.

3.

My Lady,
teach me not to hoard
the energies of my body
as in a barrel
or in a pantry,
but to consume them
and burn them all,
day by day,
for your glory
and for the good of my brothers:
without keeping back anything,
neither life nor that
which I hold most dear,
until death.

4.

May the Most Holy Virgin
present to God
these my weak
but assiduous prayers

and with their purity
may they bend the heart of
    the Eternal
always to care for us
with the eye of fatherly
    goodness.
May it please this blessed Mother
to make us worthy
of eternal glory.

Reflections

1.

I feel close and bound to
    the Son
through this Mother,
without even seeing the chains
that hold me so tight;
a thousand flames consume me;
I feel like I am dying all the time,
yet still alive. I wish I could fly
to invite all creatures
to love Jesus, to love Mary.

2.

Our Lady teaches us
with her motherhood
that the true temple of God,
the real church is our body,
where the heart is transformed
into an altar
and the brain into a pulpit.
Within us the real retreats
and the true expectations
of penance
and of prayer!
From the heart of this small
church
exclusively ours,
we manage to obtain,
with patient waiting,
the tender help
of the Blessed Virgin,
who pushes away with prudence,
serenity, and confidence
the monster of despair.

3.

In my priestly service
I have had only one model,
one still-point: Our Lady,
and I believe that
I could not have done differently.
I could not betray Mom.
I, a docile instrument
in the hands of Our Lady,
throughout my life,
wanted to do
a little cleansing of souls;
these souls I wanted to adorn
with good intentions
both by absolving,
and denying absolution.
So I would like to fly
towards Heaven
to the summons of the Blessed
Virgin
and thus I would want them,
my spiritual children, to fly
without further stumbling.
And as to prayer,

as I tried to fix
my eyes
on the eyes of the Heavenly Mother,
so I wish they would do,
my spiritual children.

The prayers and reflections of Saint Pio are taken from the volumes published by Publications Padre Pio da Pietrelcina, which we thank for allowing us to publish them.

For an in-depth study on the Marian devotion of the Saint, we recommend the book by Marcellino Iasenzaniro, *Padre Pio parla della Madonna* (*Padre Pio Speaks of Our Lady*), Publications Padre Pio da Pietrelcina, San Giovanni Rotondo (Foggia, Italy) 2006.